A Curious Catalogue
Holiday 2010

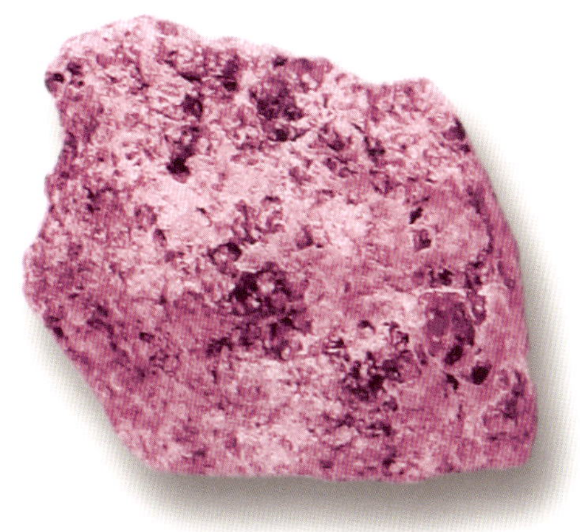

by Michael Leon

First Edition

Co-Edited by Thomas Erber
on the occasion of
Cabinet de Curiosites, Colette, Paris
Design by Dave Vander Maas

Published By Nieves
www.nievesbook.com

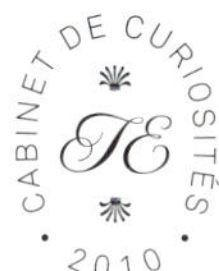

In 1983, I had a skateboard. It was navy blue with gold trucks and red wheels. I don't know where it came from. I used small rocks to set up a slalom course in my driveway. I tried to do wheelies. Not because I was aware that this was an established skateboard maneuver, but because I could do them on my bicycle. I did not know anything about the culture of skateboarding, nor did I define myself as a skateboarder. I spent the Summer moving in and out of a row of rocks. I also used the skateboard to travel to a nearby park; sometimes with a basketball under my arm. At night my skateboard leaned against the wall just inside my front door.

In 2010, I started the Curious Skateboard Company for people like me.
This is our catalogue of products.

- Michael Leon

'There is no governing body that declares any regulations on what constitutes a skateboard or the parts from which it is assembled.'

- en.wikipedia.org/wiki/Skateboard

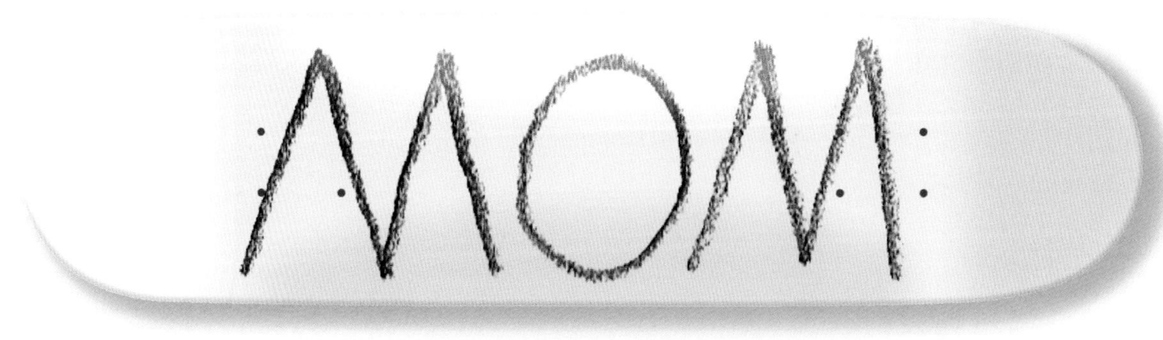

MOM / 8x32 / $49.95

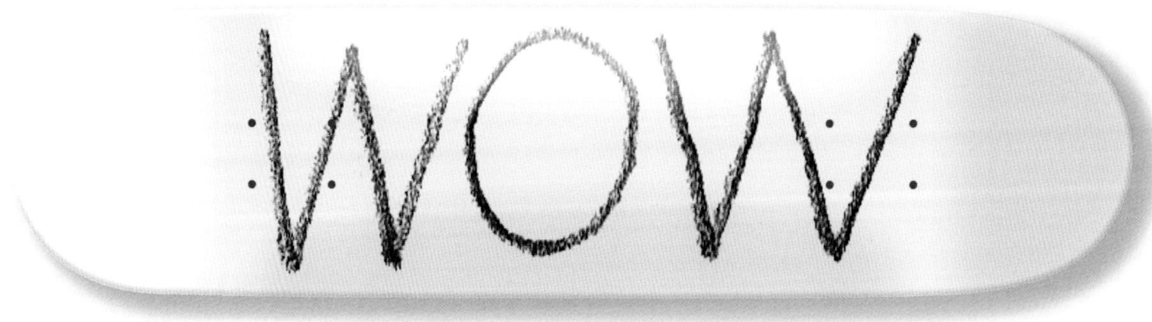

WOW / 8x32 / $59.95

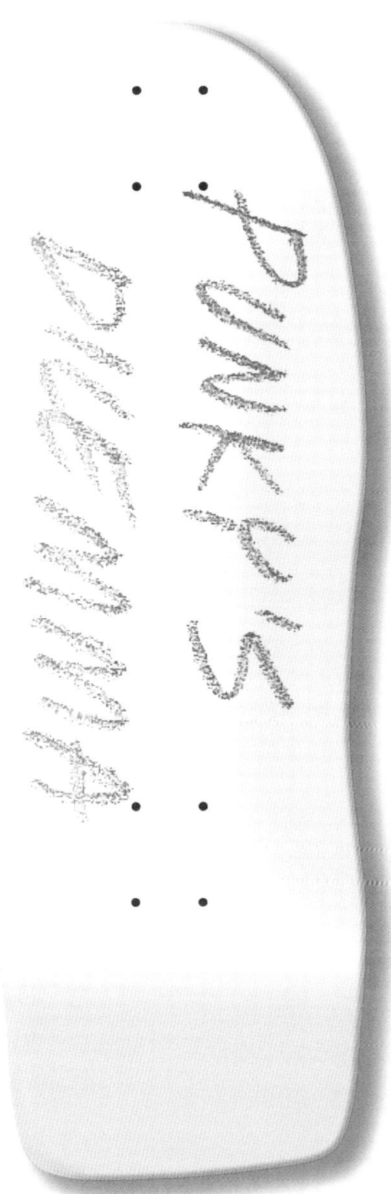

Punky's Dilemma / 10x30 / $49.95

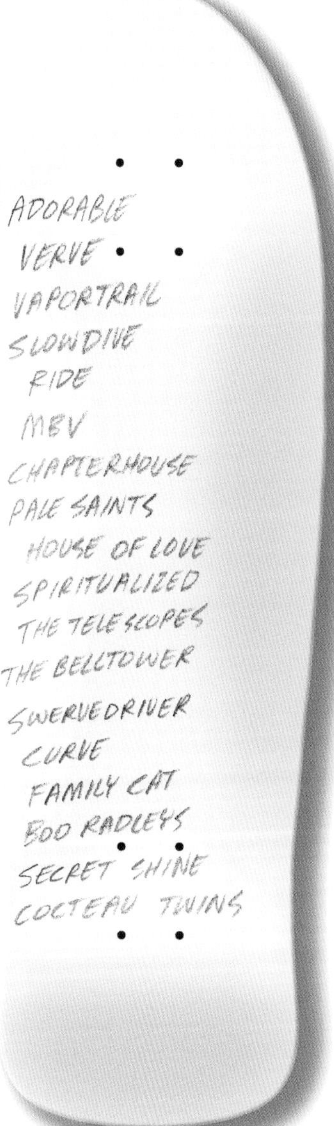

Best Friend 1 / 10x30 / $49.95

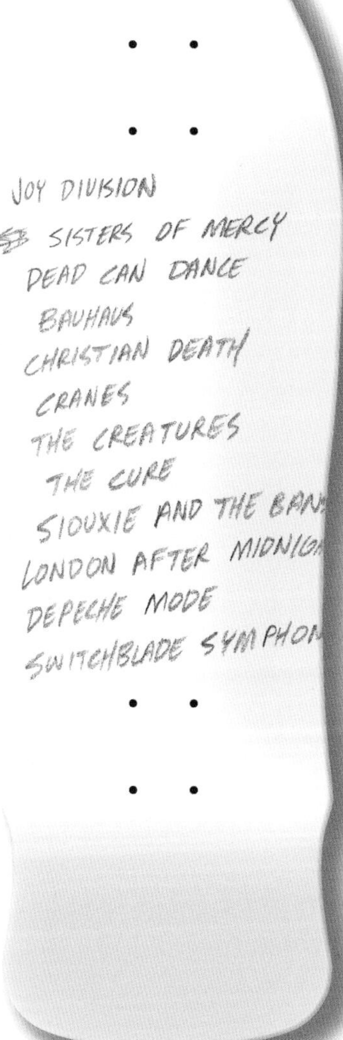

Best Friend 2 / 10x30 / $49.95

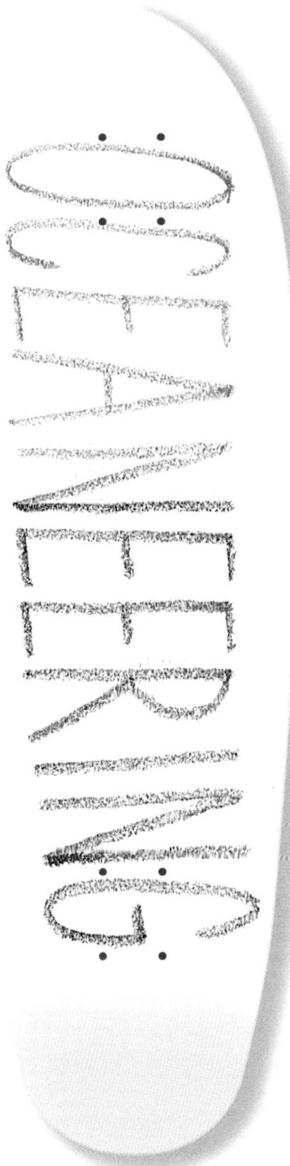

Other Options / 9x32 / $49.95

Cerulean Tower / 7x28 / $49.95

Bowery / 7x28 / $49.95

One Aldwych / 7x28 / $49.95

Roosevelt / 7x28 / $49.95

THE
COORS
LIGHT
BREWING
COMPANY
IS
STOKED
TO BE A
SPONSOR
OF
THE
CANADIAN
SNOWBOARD
TEAM

Second Life / 10.5x31 / $49.95

WE
PEELED
THE
"BONELESS"
STICKERS
OFF OF
FROZEN
CHICKEN
AND
STUCK
THEM ON
OUR
BOARDS

Boneless / 10x29 / $49.95

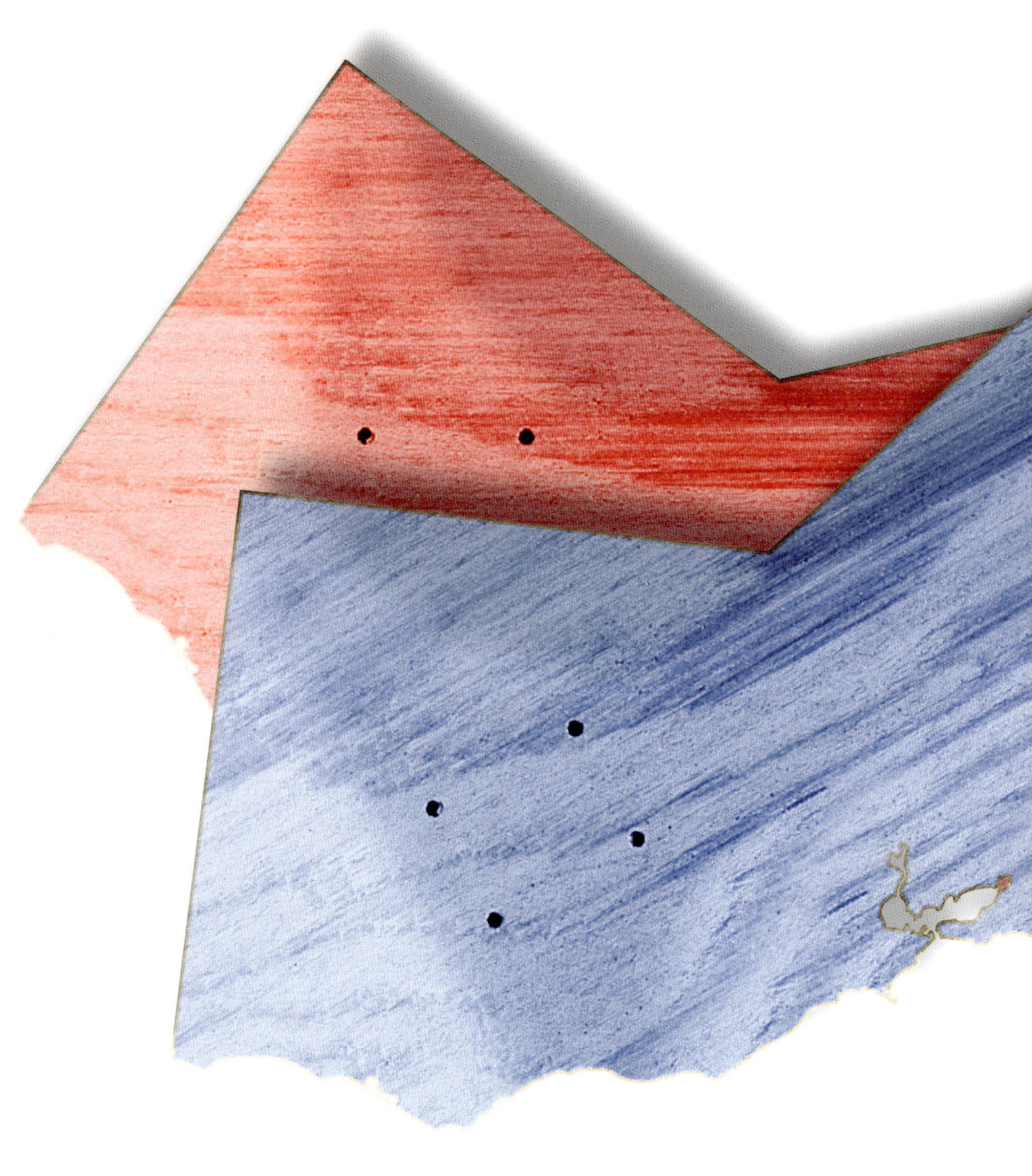

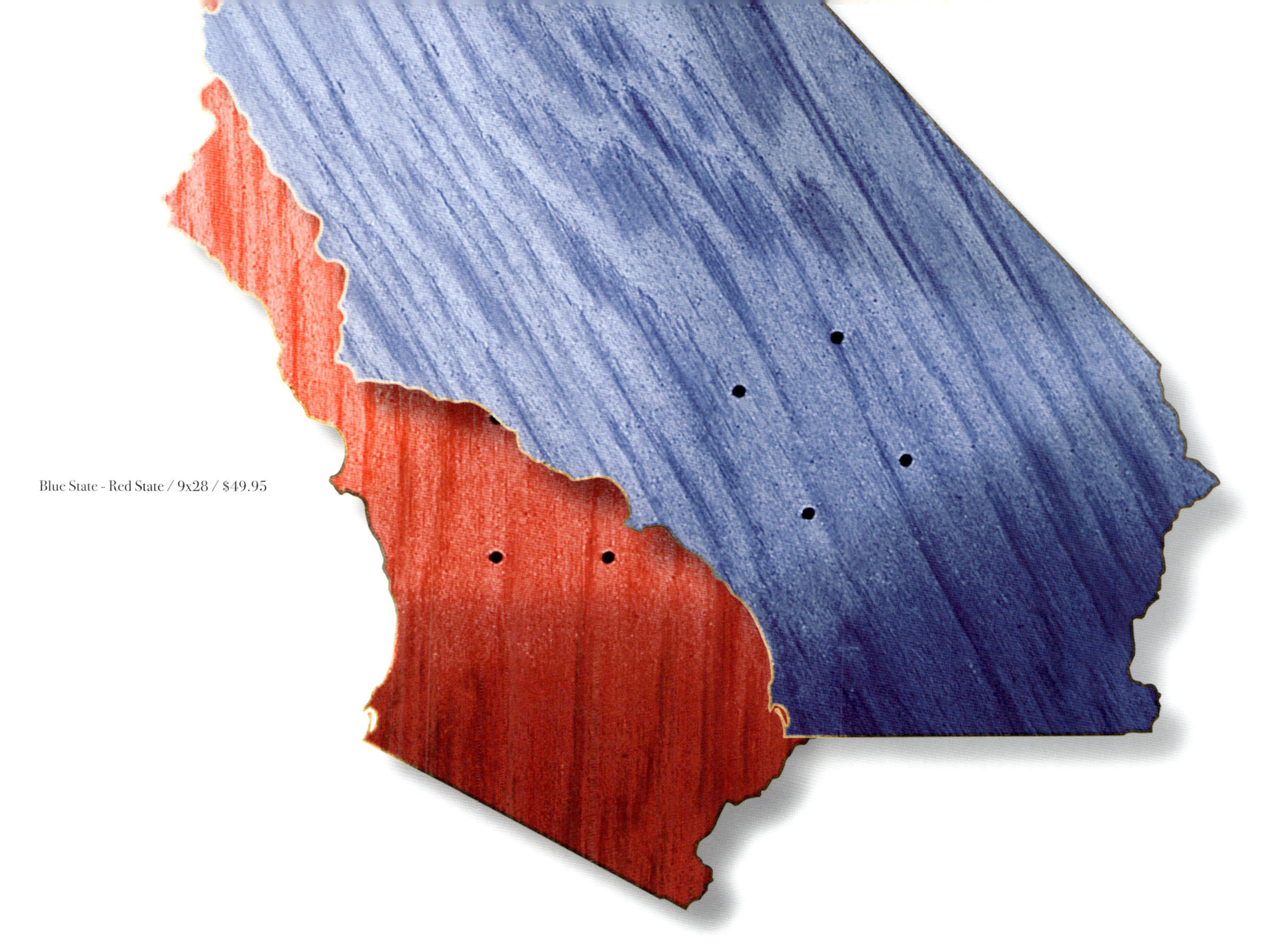

Blue State - Red State / 9x28 / $49.95

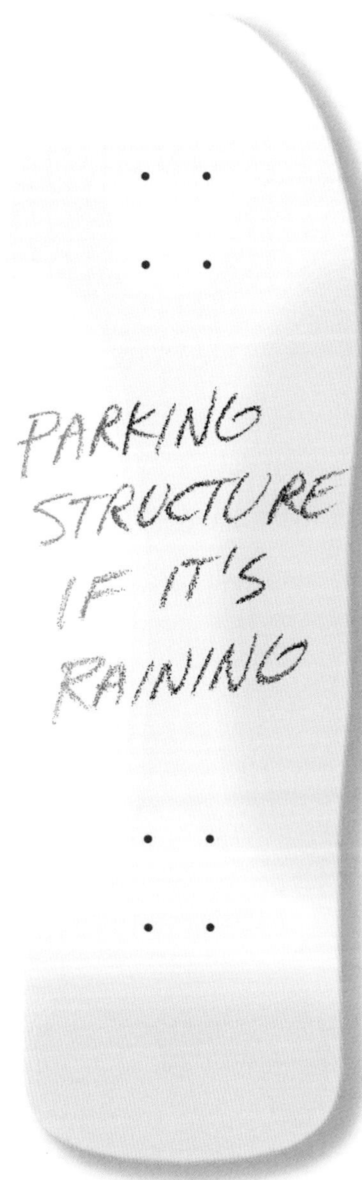

Parking Structure / 10x30 / $49.95

THIS IS A
MAP THAT
WILL TAKE
YOU
SOMEWHERE.
BUT WHEN
YOU GET
THERE YOU
WONT REALLY
KNOW WHERE
YOU ARE

Smithson / 10x30 / $49.95

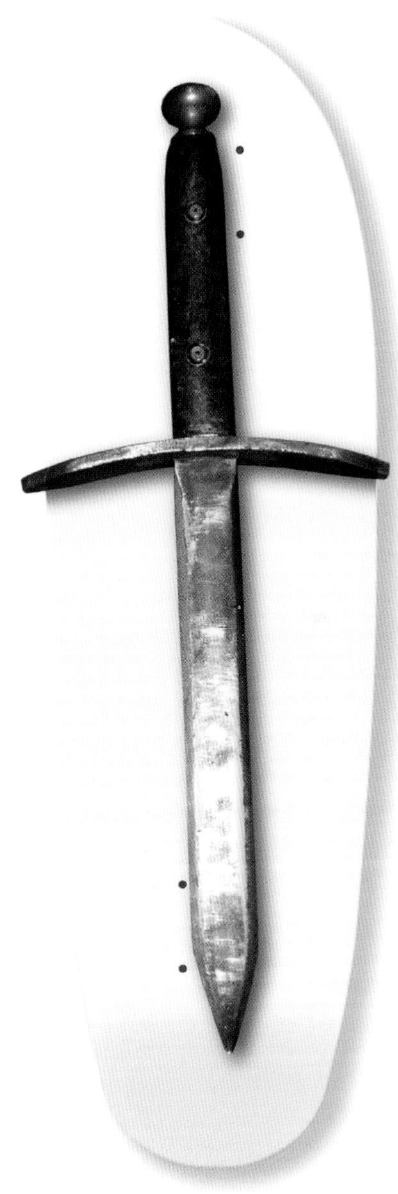

Dagger / 7x27 / $49.95

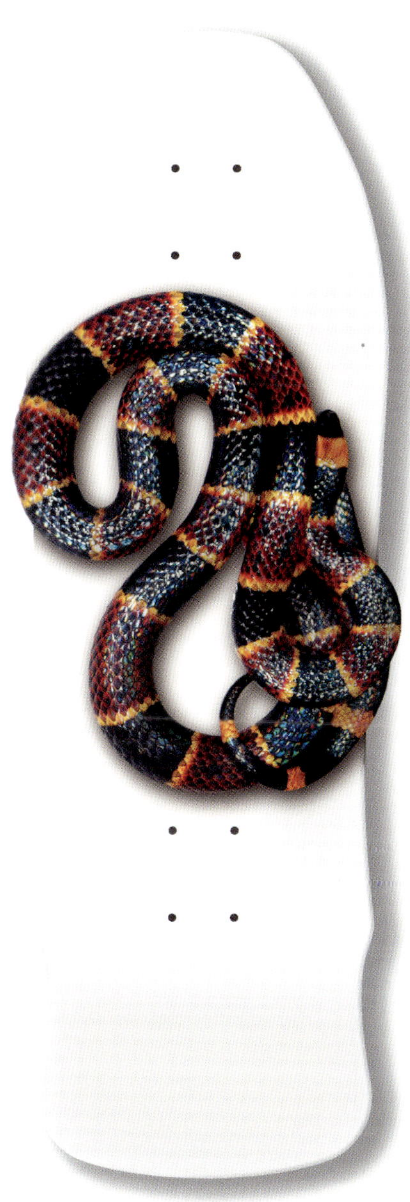

Serpent / 10x29 / $49.95

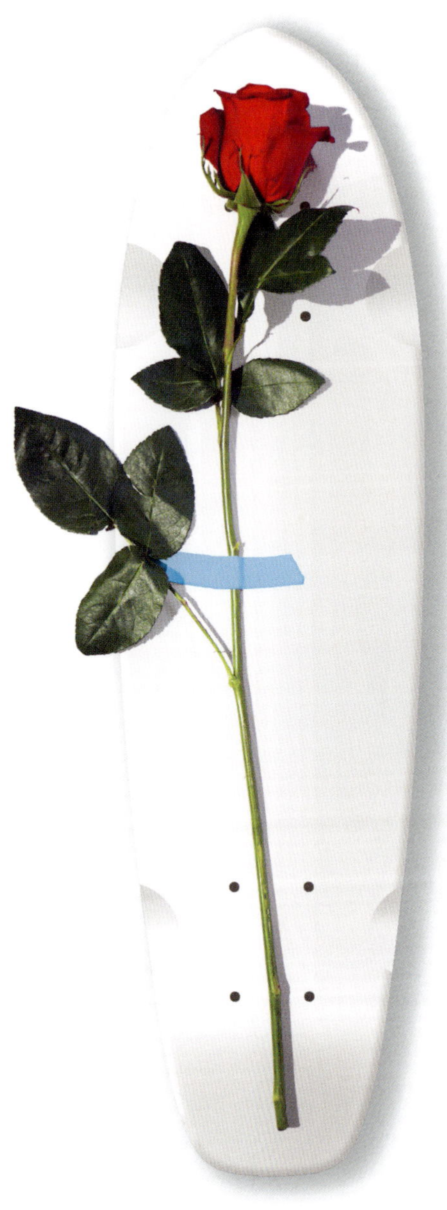

Rose / 7.5x28 / $59.95

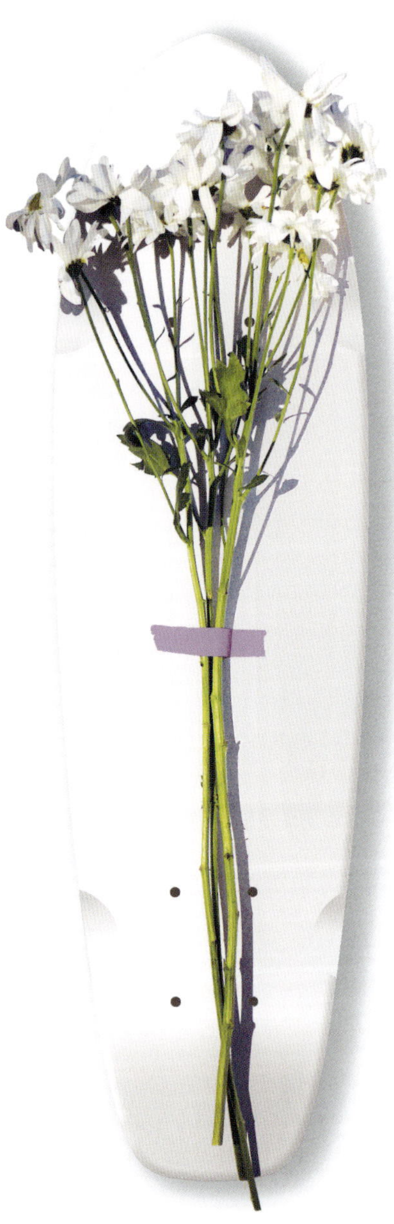

Daisies / 7.5x28 / $49.95

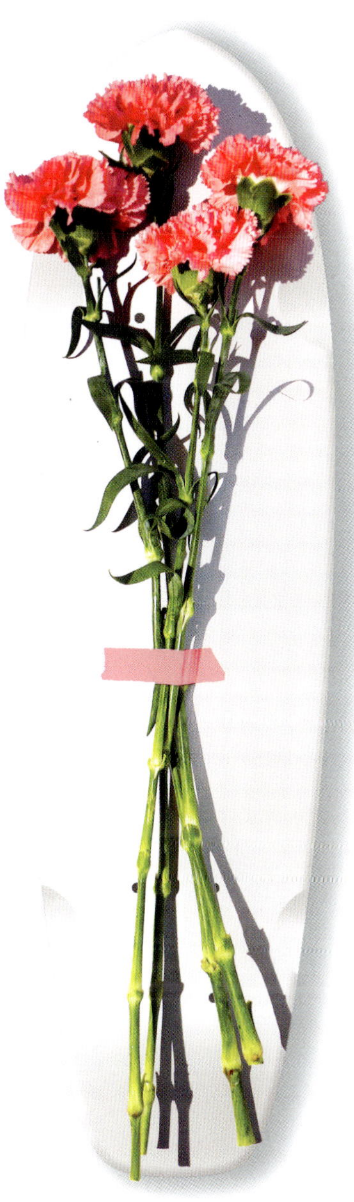

Carnations / 7.5x28 / $49.95

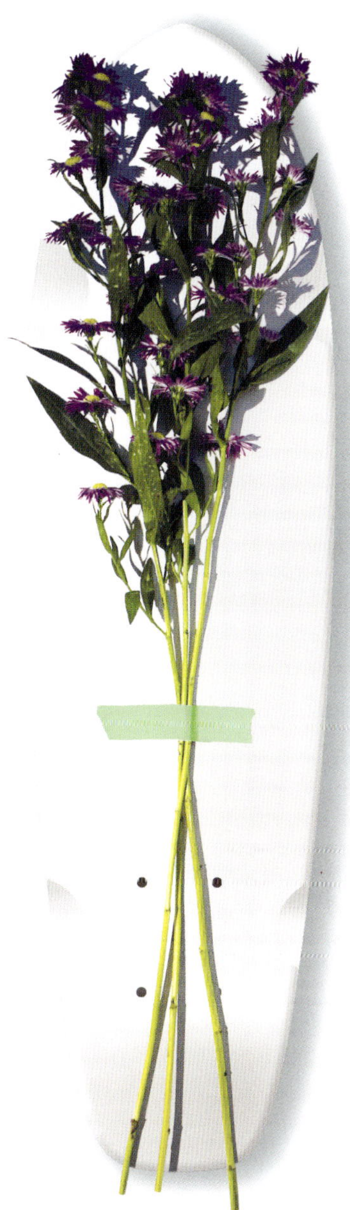

Violets / 7.5x28 / $49.95

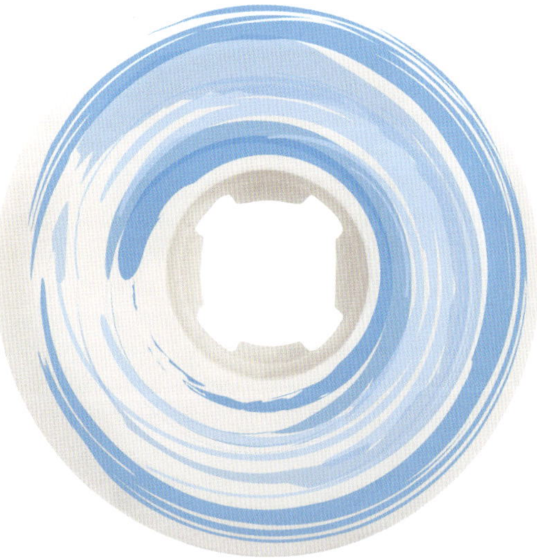

Tubes / 54mm / $34.99

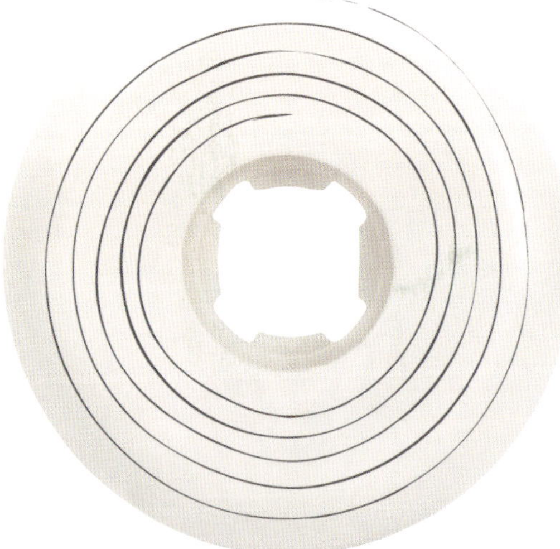

Finelines / 53mm / $34.99

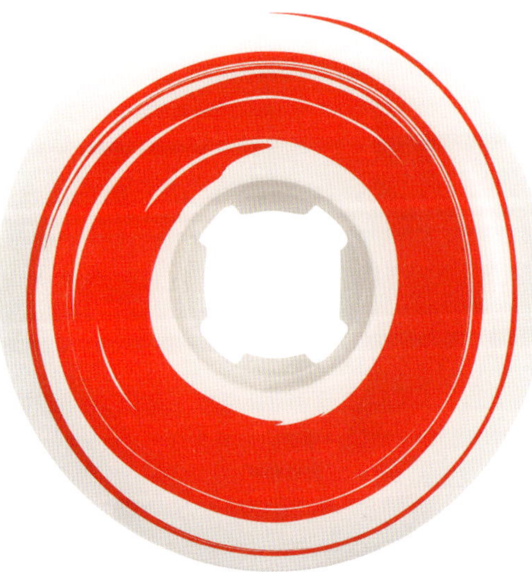

Reds / 52mm / $34.99

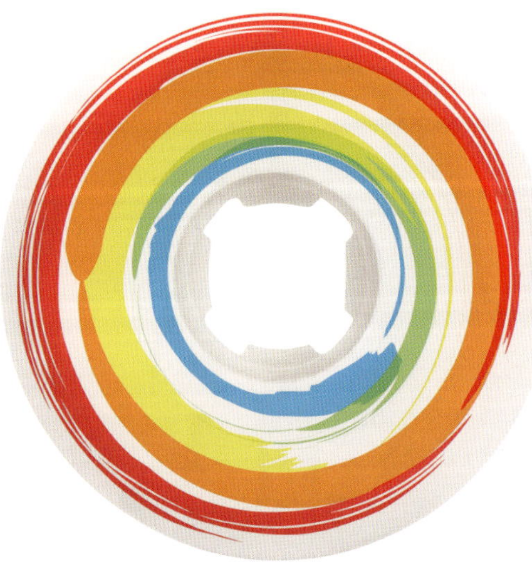

Spectrums / 51mm / $34.99

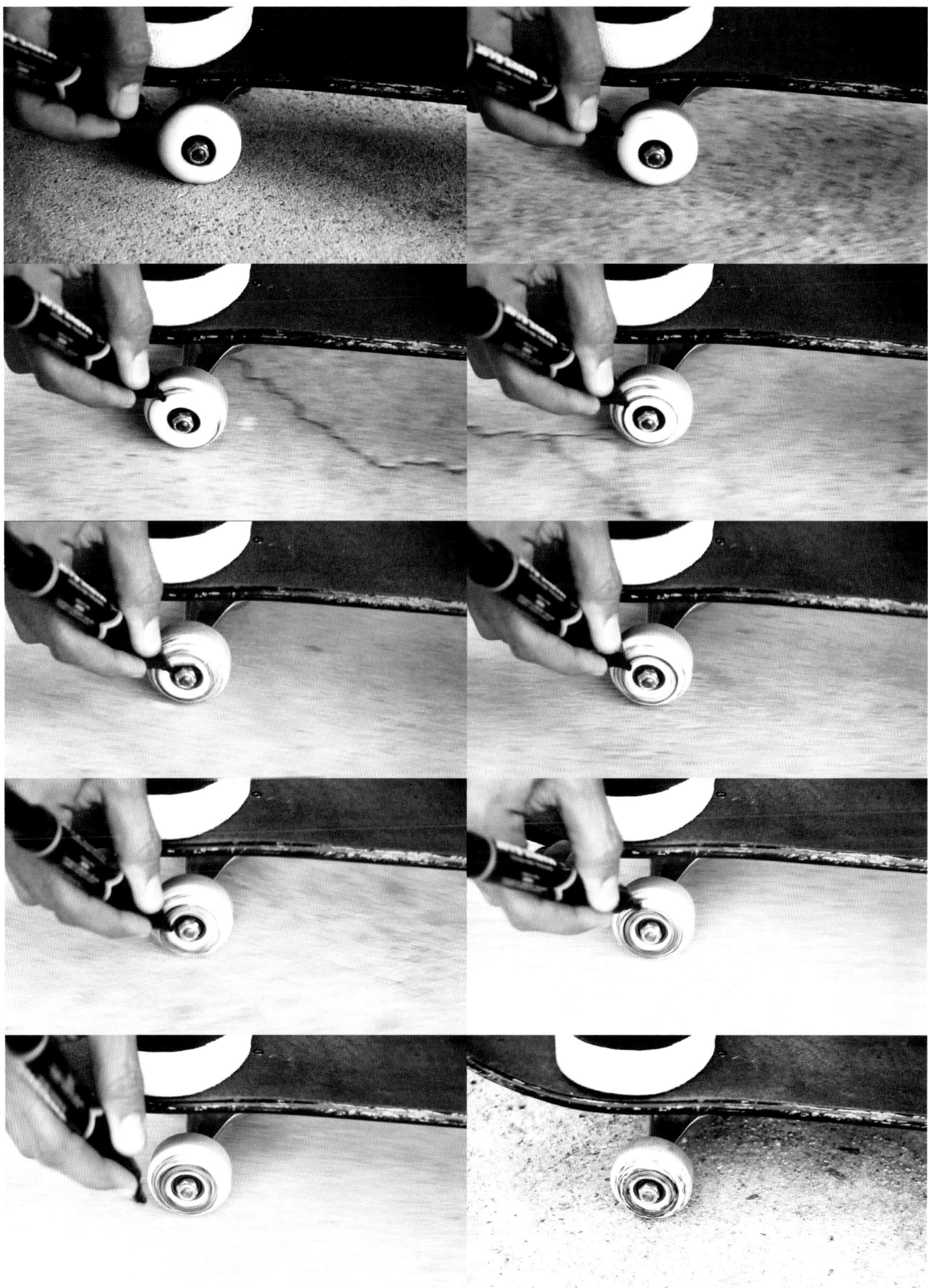

Photos: Paul Stec

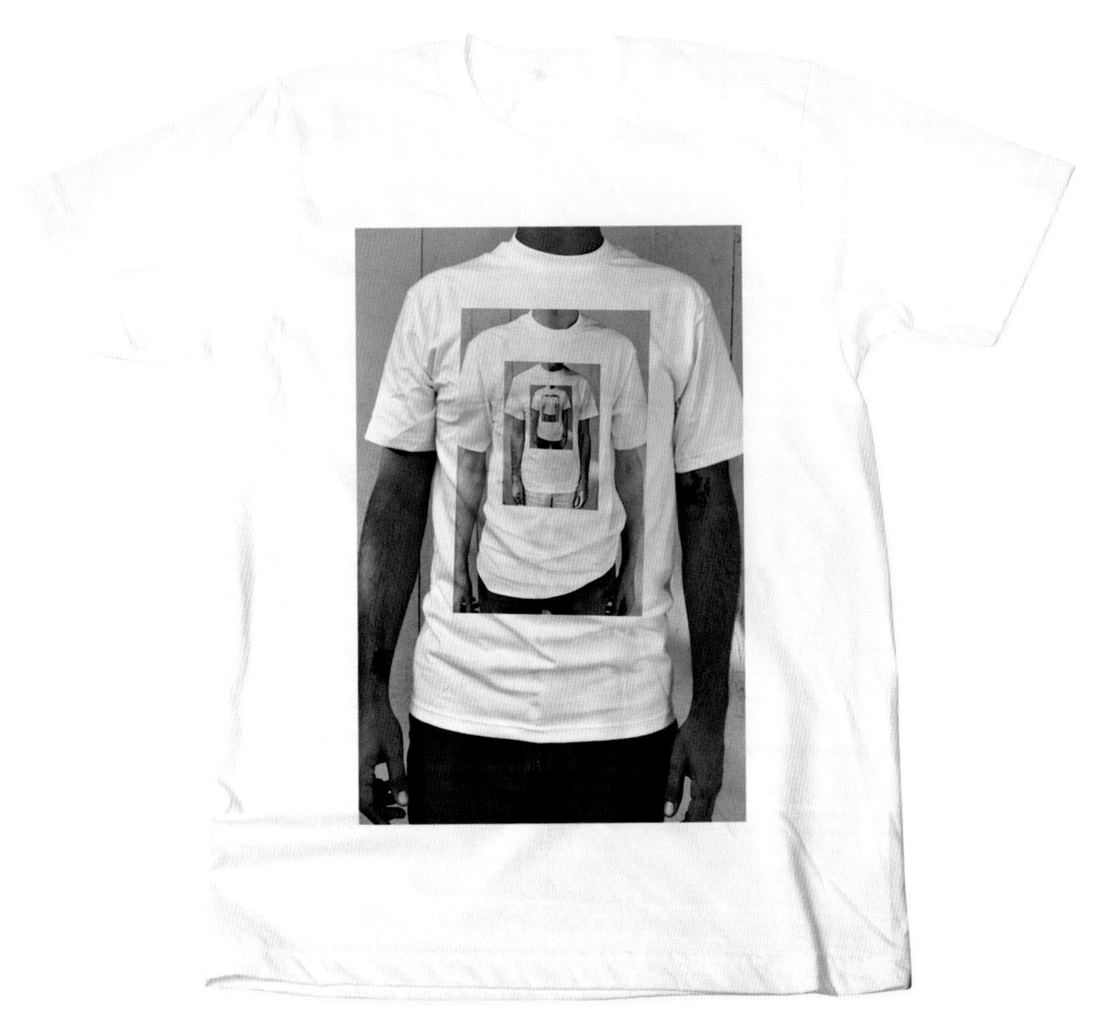

Front Door / S-XL / $24.99

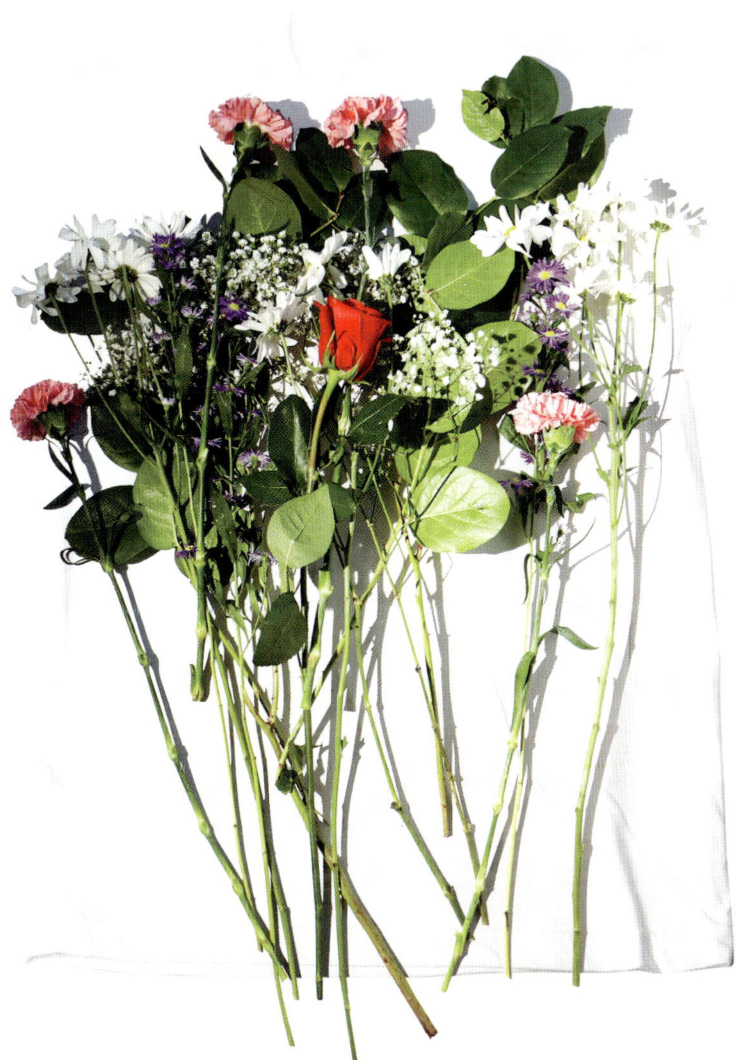

Flowers / S-XL / $24.99

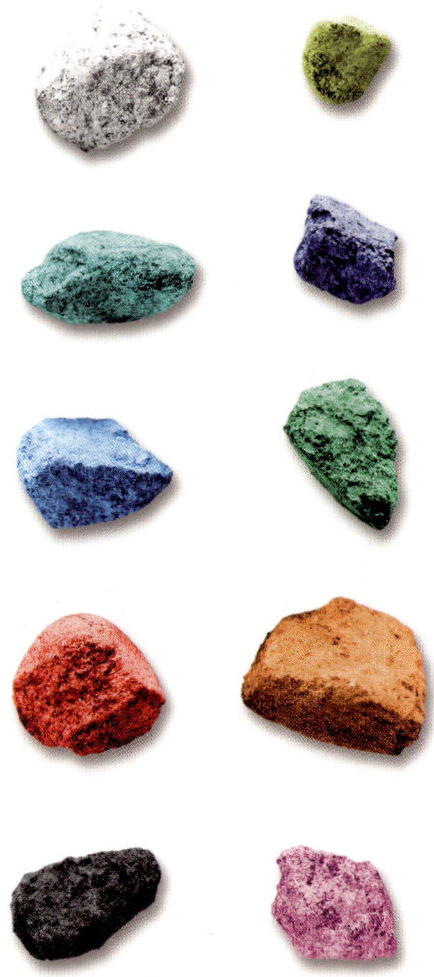

Hand Painted Slalom Stones / Set of 10 / $29.95